C000291868

CAPE POETRY PAPERBACKS

ADRIAN MITCHELL
POEMS

by the same author

poems
Out Loud
Ride the Nightmare

novels
If You See Me Comin'
The Bodyguard

play
Tyger

Adrian Mitchell

POEMS

JONATHAN CAPE
THIRTY BEDFORD SQUARE LONDON

FIRST PUBLISHED 1964
© 1964 BY ADRIAN MITCHELL
REISSUED IN THIS FORMAT 1969
REPRINTED 1971, 1972

JONATHAN CAPE LTD
30 BEDFORD SQUARE, LONDON WC1

ISBN 0 224 61775 3

Condition of Sale

This book is sold subject to the condition that it
shall not, by way of trade or otherwise, be lent,
re-sold, hired out, or otherwise circulated without the publisher's prior consent, in any form
of binding or cover other than that in which
it is published and without a similar condition
including this condition being imposed on the
subsequent purchaser.

Printed in Great Britain by
Fletcher & Son Ltd, Norwich
and bound by
Richard Clay (The Chaucer Press) Ltd, Bungay, Suffolk

Contents

Acknowledgments

Poems in this book have previously appeared in A.B.C. Television, *The Animal's Friend*, *An Anthology of Modern Verse, 1940–1960*, the B.B.C. Third Programme, *Crux*, *Delta*, *Departure*, *International Socialism*, *The Isis*, *Jazz Poems*, *The Kenyon Review*, *The London Magazine*, *New Departures*, *New Writing*, *The New Yorker*, *Oxford Poetry, 1954*, *Oxford Poetry, 1955*, the *P.E.N. Anthology, 1961*, *Stand*, *The Times Literary Supplement*, *Tribune* and *Trio*. Four of the poems appeared in a Fantasy Press pamphlet.

A selection of these poems, together with the libretto of the opera 'The Ledge', gained a £200 Gregory Award in 1961.

Most people ignore most poetry

because

most poetry ignores most people

People

Goodbye

He breathed in air, he breathed out light.
Charlie Parker was my delight.

The Institution

The crazy talkers in my head
Steal lights and moments when they can;
Beat at the windows to be fed
Or listen to the sounds of rain.
They stroll, they shout at passing Man,
And in extremes they form a plan
To drown at night, or catch a train.

Simple as glass, they wander through
The colours of my twenty years
Singing and whispering the true
And false of all my private cares;
Inflated songs that shrink to fears.
My chest is thick, so no one hears
The lovely mute who kicks and tears ...

Crusoe Dying in England

Always the seagulls cry on me
Weak from the waves. They tell me tales,
Say: 'Now you breathe the English sky;
You have been rescued from the toils
Of the black island.' All the day
They speak fair times. But constantly
Caged in my chest a huge fowl wails
And screams the truth above the lie:
England is drowned. Old age despoils
My senses. I am cast away.

My body is a breathing weight
Obscenely formed to be my shame.
I cannot show it to the light
But hide it in my hollow room;
For now the rooted traps are set,
The springs are sour and my estate
Is lost to me. I have no name.
Thick grow the poison weeds, no flight
Is possible. The branches loom
Shining above with lazy sweat.

Fruit hangs and drops upon the hut
Endlessly from heavy trees.
I have no will to hook or net
Fantastic fish I used to prize.
Shuddering skies melt in the heat
To soak my limbs. My heart is shut
And locked to hope. My silly knees
Kissing the earth, let me forget
The ghosts who turn before my eyes,
Companions of sea and street.

We would go, swaggering and fine,
To rake the taverns of a port.
My storming friends, we loved in vain
For now your eyes are all put out.
Shackled along the rusty chains
Of thought, you are not truly mine.
Captives, but you will not be taught
To sing, or move, or speak again.
Bad air invades me from without.
My friends lie sullen in my brains.

Crusoe? I am some other thing,
A city caught in evil days
Of plague and fire : I am a throng
Of shaking men : I am a race
Undone by fear, for I was born
In a cursed country. Who is King?
Who is the ruler of this shattered place
Myself? The Bible God? But strong
Crusoe is dead. I have no face;
An old mad god, my powers gone.

Canine Canto

Dogs thurber through the whitman grass
On wild shakespearean excursions.
They have no waugh or corneille class
In their laurence sterne diversions.
They sniff blake blooms and patchen weeds,
They have no time for strindberg doom,
Or walks on firm jane austen leads,
Formal pope gardens or the baudelaire room.
As for donne love, while going it,
They lawrence without knowing it.

I Passed for Sane

If I'd been born without a mind
I would be happy, tame and kind.
People came, saying good things,
So many people, saying good things.
I hid my eyes under my skin
And so they never saw right in.

Song about Mary

Mary sat on a long brown bench
Reading *Woman's Own* and *She*,
Then a slimy-haired nit with stripes on his collar
Said: 'What's the baby's name to be?'

She looked across to Marks and Spencers
Through the dirty window pane,
'I think I'll call him Jesus Christ,
It's time he came again.'

The clerk he banged his ledger
And he called the Cruelty Man
Saying: 'This bird thinks she's the mother of Christ,
Do what you bleeding well can.'

They took Mary down to the country
And fed her on country air,
And they put the baby in a Christian home
And he's much happier there.

For if Jesus came to Britain
He would turn its dizzy head,
You'd see him arrested at the next sit-down
And he'd raise the poor from the dead.

So if you have a little baby
Make sure it's a legitimate child,
Bind down his limbs with insurance
And he'll grow up meek and mild.
      Meek and mild ... meek and mild ... meek and mild.

The Accountant in his Bath

The accountant dried his imperfect back
As he stood in the sinking water —
'In ten years' time I'll be dead as cork,
No sooner, no later.

'Numbers display more muscle every day,
They multiply while I'm asleep.
When I fall to pieces they won't even see,
They'll keep on adding each other up.

'I know the numbers, each has a colour,
Twenty-three is olive green,
Five's a comedian (all have characters),
One is God and eight's the Queen.

'But I was never envious of numbers,
Watching them replace each other;
Like the grim wolves, not one remembers
His fading father.

'Passionless, lean, their armies march,
Invade more ledgers, take more men alive;
But they're not free to run or lurch
Each to his private grave.'

Patches of water shrank inside the bath.
Confident in the immortal numbers
He heard his wife's amazing laugh;
'I love her,' he said, as he pulled on his pyjamas.

For my Son

'The next best thing to the human tear' ... advertising slogan
for an eyewash.

The next best thing to the human tear
Is the human smile
Which beams at us reflected white
For a lunar while.
But smiles congeal. Two eyes alight
With water cannot glow for long,
And a better thing than the human tear
Is the human song.

If cigarette or city burn
The smoke breaks into air.
So your breath, cries and laughter turn
And are abandoned there.
Once I had everything to learn
And thought each book had pretty pages.
Now I don't even trust the sun
Which melts like butter through the ages.

Nevertheless, crack-voiced I'll sing
For you, who drink the generous light
Till, fat as happiness, you sing
Your gay, immortal appetite.
I bring you air, food, grass and rain,
Show you the breast where you belong.
You take them all and sing again
Your human song.

Buddy Bolden

He bust through New Orleans
On his cornet night and day,
Buddy kept on stompin'
Till he was put away.

He chose his girls like kings do
And drank like earth was hell,
But when they tried to cut him
He played like Gabriel.

The notes shot out his cornet
Like gobs come off a ship.
You felt the air get tighter
And then you heard it rip.

They threw him in the bughouse
And took away his horn.
He hadn't felt so mean since
The day that he was born.

Some say corn liquor done it
Or ruttin' a bad whore
But I guess he blew so much out
He couldn't think no more.

The Clown is Dead

Children must learn that fairy tales are lies,
Faces are masks, and peace is out of reach.
I stare into the clown's unwinking eyes
Discovering the child they could not teach.

Though he rode out of childhood cheerfully
He left that forest for the open lands
In fear of other men. He could not see
If they held knives or flowers in their hands.

Seeing the animals, he learnt to speak
Solemnly to them, and at length remove
Their simple terrors; for if he was weak
In anything, it was not in his love.

*   *   *

Death came to him when he was young
And he stuck out his scarlet tongue.
He went to death when he was old:
'Take me,' he said, 'it's turning cold.'

The bearded lady and the tattooed man
Played cards inside his caravan.
We sat around his tousled bed,
Shivered with him till he was dead.

That was a quiet way, to fade,
For him, who loved to sit astride
The high giraffe in the parade,
With blare and bang of brass and hide.

It was a quiet way to fall.
Into the ring he used to come
With a high tragic caterwaul –
And he always fell upon his bum.

*　*　*

What was the colour of his mind?
It was a prism, casting lights,
Changing, revolving in the wind
Of roaring days and storming nights.

Our elephants of laughter strode
Across his earthy doubletalk.
He goaded them to a stampede
And shot them with a popping cork.

He met tired walkers every day,
They were ill with travelling.
His songs enchanted them to stay:
They learnt to sing.

What's left? A clown of empty cloth,
A crumpled rainbow on the floor
Of a black cupboard. The destroying moth
Nests in the shapeless hat he wore.

What remains with any man?
There is no answer.
In this circus no one can
Dance, but he was a dancer.

He had no children, but I would
Stand as his son, to keep his name
And watch his footsteps take the road
Of prancing beyond praise or blame.

*   *   *

The gentle unicorn has gone away.
The dodo, poker-faced and knockabout
Saw that its tail was turning grey,
Ate up the door and waddled out.

In his good time he followed these
Moonstruck and happy monsters. All
His laughter has gone with him, and like these
He is extinct or mythical.

And he is fabulously still;
The greasepaint grin wiped off his face
By lightly sliding hands, until
The naked lips grin in its place.

*   *   *

In his hands put an apple from a tree,
Bury him deep so no one can see,
For a dead man's smile tears the whole heart down.
The clown is dead. Long live the clown.

Riddle

Their tongues are knives, their forks are hands and feet.
They feed each other through their skins and eat
Religiously the spiced, symbolic meat.
The loving oven cooks them in its heat—
Two curried lovers on a rice-white sheet.

All Fools' Day

A man sits counting the days of spring,
His hands may tremble but his mind won't stir,
And one thought runs through all his watching:
'I would have burnt my heart for her.

'If she had recognized my face
As I knew hers, and listened to me sing,
I would have left the careless human race
For one hour of her careful loving.

'When spring swings round again, and I am here,
I will forget the terrors of her voice —
But I would stay with terror at my ear
And burn my heart, if I had any choice.'

Poker

Bluff is the game: the only hand
You ever hold is in your mind.
If your luck jumps you must restrain
Your muscles, or the moves you planned
Will be as open as the wind.
Pick up the cards and deal again.

Remember that opponents place
Their bets according to your eyes
Which may inform against your brain;
But narks are easy to erase.
Beginners have to pay the price,
Pick up the cards and deal again.

Bluff is the game, but then you say
Your losses never seem to fade.
Then quit, when all your debts are paid.
You might find, on a lucky day,
Somebody who has never played.
Pick up the cards and deal again.

The Child at Night

The legends of the giant nights
Fall round this child as shadows swell
Over his island. All the tender lights
Which could destroy the pattern of the spell
Will come no more till morning.

'Walk on a grave : below he feels
Your pressure; from his agony
His brittle arms will rise to grasp your heels,
Will draw you through the earth for company
And hold you there till morning.'

Such stories ride across his land
While the dead rule and with dark paws
Drag at his heartstrings; but the sun's white hand
Will mend his wounds and break the narrow claws
Which hold him till the morning.

The Observer

A tattooed Irishman still
Shaking from his pneumatic drill.
  From his mouth
  Saunters sweet talk
  As he stretches the chained spoon
  To his mug of tea again.
  Talk as sweet and warm as tea
  Floats in bubbles from his mouth.
  As he counts fivepence he's reminded
  That his working life has ended.
  Bubbles burst. His tongue's light tune
  Stumbles and does not rise. Deep in his belly
  The molten tea solidifies.
  His tall face lowers slowly
  Like a red wall collapsing in the rain.

A young Guards officer
Shaking with long-imprisoned anger.
  From his mouth
  Marches, in step, his conversation
  As he taps a silver plate
  With his menthol cigarette.
  Talk as white and soft as smoke
  Pours from his educated mouth.
  His Colonel claims that the Brigade
  Might well recruit the unemployed.
  The young man's facial veins inflate,
  His talk moves at the double, sweating,
  Mad keen, but disciplined at that,
  As his whole face opens letting
  Free a smile bright as a bayonet.

23

In the café and the mess
A liberal hears what each man says.
   He notes the navvy's imagination
   And he smiles.
   Notes the Guard's well-drilled conversation
   And he smiles.
   With memories of Wimbledon
   He says under his pleasant breath :
   'Why don't both men just jump the net,
   Shake hands, and say the class war's won?'
   He lights a Woodbine from a Ronson.
   His eyes bulge, large with vision,
   Seeing both sides of every question,
   One with his left eye,
   One with his right,
   The cross-eyed, doomed hermaphrodite.

Loyal and Religious

Another Prince is Born

Fire off the bells, ring out wild guns,
Switch on the sun for the son of sons.
For loyal rubbernecks to wait
Stick a notice on the gate.
Thrill to frill and furbelow,
God Save Sister Helen Rowe.
Lord Evans, Peel, Hall and Sir John
Guard the cot he dribbles on.
An angel in a Hunter jet
Circles round his bassinette.
Inform *The Times*, *Debrett*, *Who's Who*,
Better wake C. Day Lewis too.

Comes the parade of peers and peasants,
The Queen bears children, they bear presents—
Balls and toy guardsmen, well-trained parrots,
A regal rattle (eighteen carats),
And one wise man with myrrh-oiled hair
Brings a six-foot teddy bear
From the Birmingham Toy Fair.

Lying in State

He's dead. Into the vault and out
Shuffles the reverent conga.
With his intestines taken out
He will stay sweeter longer.

Quite Apart from the Holy Ghost

I remember God as an eccentric millionaire,
Locked in his workshop, beard a cloud of foggy-coloured hair,
Making the stones all different, each flower and disease,
Putting the Laps in Lapland, making China for the Chinese,
Laying down the Lake of Lucerne as smooth as blue-grey lino,
Wearily inventing the appendix and the rhino,
Making the fine fur for the mink, fine women for the fur,
Man's brain a gun, his heart a bomb, his conscience – a blur.

Christ I can see much better from here,
And Christ upon the Cross is clear.
Jesus is stretched like the skin of a kite
Over the Cross, he seems in flight
Sometimes. At times it seems more true
That he is meat nailed up alive and pain all through.
But it's hard to see Christ for priests. That happens when
A poet engenders generations of advertising men.

England

Remember Suez?

England, unlike junior nations,
Wears officers' long combinations.
So no embarrassment was felt
By the Church, the Government or the Crown.
But I saw the Thames like a grubby old belt
And England's trousers falling down.

The Fox

A fox among the shadows of the town,
Should I surrender to the arms of man?
  On the blank icehills lies in wait
  The fighting cold who has thrown down
  His challenge. I'll not imitate
  The feline compromise. I scan
  With warring eyes the servile fate
Of animals who joined the heated town.

Lean-hearted lions in the concrete zoo
Grow bellies, tendons slacken in pale hide,
  Their breath slows to a dying pace.
  Their keepers love them? Tell me who
  Would cage his love in such a place,
  Where only fish are satisfied?
  The keeper has a huntsman's face,
His grasping love would kill me in the zoo.

A scavenger throughout the snowing wind
I peel the sweet bark from the frozen tree
Or trap the bird with springing jaws.
The sun retreats out of my mind.
How could I give this waking pause
When death's my sleeping company?
Mad empty, licking at my sores,
I howl this bitter and unloving wind.

Furious in this savage winter day
The crimson riders hounded me from birth
Through landscapes built of thorn and stone.
Though I must be their sudden prey,
Torn to my terror's skeleton,
Or go to the forgotten earth;
I will have hunted, too, alone,
I will have wandered in my handsome day.

Four seasons wrestle me, I throw them all
And live to tumble with another year
In love or battle. I'll not fly
From mindless elements and fall
A victim to the keeper's lie.
The field is mine; but still I fear
Strong death, my watching enemy,
Though seasons pass and I survive them all.

The Beggar

The beggar shouts his martial wares:
'One bad eye and one wooden leg.
Now is the time for cash, not stares,
I am not rotting here to beg.

Who'll buy the north wind of the mind?
A fascinating pet. You'll find
  It's got a fist like a mallet
  Voice like a cistern
  Teeth like granite
  And an arm like a piston.
Sometimes it strays abroad for nights
But hunger brings it home. It bites
Only its master and his kind.
Your brain's the field, it is the mole.
Who buy my devil or my soul?

'One wooden leg and one bad eye.
Then I danced, but now I flick
The woodlouse from my sewn-up thigh.
Watch them both and take your pick.
Once I was unique, alive,
Daubed with love you'd not believe.
  Then I saw the stars by day
  Looking from a well.
  Now the best that I can pray
  Is that my other eye should fail.
They sell you tickets to the moon,
I curse you with the sucking fly;
But who, bar me, hawks in this town
A dead branch and an evil eye?'

Fascist Speaker

Armoured like a rhinoceros
He hurls his tons into the crowd.
From half a dozen minds he rips
Triangles of flesh and blood.

33

Six shouts, six cardboard banners rise
Daubed with slogans saying Pain,
But wilt and tear in the hundredfold
Applause of men as mild as rain.

Man at Large

Observe that man and see the lust
Bulging his serge as he cons a bust.
If he had to go cannibal he would eat
Only blonde secretarial meat.
His wife and his house and his brain are dim.
He didn't invent sex. Sex invented him.
He remembers a girl whose mouth was all
Like a cocktail cherry, and was smooth and cool.

Sulking down Wardour Street he goes,
Dreams in his head, corns on his toes.
But what would he do without feet? Fall down.
Where would he be without eyes? In a dark town.
Without hands? Unable to hold a knife,
A coin, a bottle or his wife.
Though his feet, eyes, hands, shuffle, stare and cling,
He falls down, is in the dark, cannot hold anything.

South Kensington is much Nicer

London, you hurt me. You're the girl
With hair fresh-permed and every curl
A gold ring in its proper place,
But spread across your poker face

A net of scars. A dress of smoke,
Your body an unfinished joke.
I love you, but I cannot sing
That money-splendoured hair is everything.
For I've walked through the alleys of Poison Town,
They led me up, they led me down.
The colour of the air was brown.

Look at the View

Like the memory of a long-dead clerical uncle
Reclines St Paul's Cathedral
In the blue smoke from London's frying-pan.
Climb to the dome, and then you can
Watch the dull length of Blackfriar's Bridge.
See the flat girl approach the edge,
Jump, fall, splash, vanish, struggle, cease.
Do you bet she'll be saved by the River Police
Who ride the tides in a humming launch?
Or an oil millionaire without a paunch
Will dive and take her wet to lunch?
Save her and leave her, and she'll be seen
Next day on the bridge near that tarnished tureen
St Paul's Cathedral, glowering in the rain.
She will take off her shoes and fall again.

Reply to a Canvasser

Cats are spies for something dark.
Rabbits are wiped out.
Captain Cousteau scares the shark
With an underwater shout.

Snakes slide over jagged ground
Making the same sound as grass.
Elephants are pushed around.
Fish are hooked, or circle worlds of glass.

Hyenas have a nervous laugh,
Corruption is their only need.
Worms get fat, then cut in half.
A dog's a footman on a lead.

I'd rather be a stag at bay
Daubed in colours brown and gory,
Or any creature any day
Than be a bloody Tory.

The Swan

The anger of the swan
Burns black
Over ambitious eyes.

The power of the swan
Flexes steel wings
To batter feeble air.

The beauty of the swan
Is the sermon
Preached between battles.

Put Down Daddy's Magazine

John was six. The cat was fat.
In a pretty picture book
The cat sat, bleeding on the mat.

Johnny gave the cat a pat,
Stood and watched the carving cook.
John was six. The cat was fat.

Cat scratched Johnny. That was that.
By the knife that Johnny took
The cat sat, bleeding on the mat.

After playing tit for tat
Johnny took a second look.
John was six. The cat was fat.

Johnny stared and stared and sat
In his cosy fire-side nook.
The cat sat bleeding on the mat.

When they came into the flat
Mama cried and Papa shook.
John was six. The cat was fat.
The cat sat, bleeding, on the mat.

Ode to Money

Man-eater, woman-eater, brighter than tigers,
Lover and killer in my pocket,
In your black sack I'm one of the vipers.
Golden-eyed mother of suicide,
Your photo's in my heart's gold locket.

You make me warm, you keep me cool,
You cure the terrifying dream.
Nature and art await your call.
Money, don't lead me to milk and honey
But a land of drambuie and icebergs of cream.

The Palm Court Planet's orchestra whines
The Money Spangled Money
And The Red Money. In my silver chains
I always stand when I hear the band
Play Money Save the Money.

From Riches to Riches

The man of the people told the people he was one of them.
After five champagne years the people crowned him King of
    Phlegm.
High priest of steel and washing machines, see where Mac-
    millan stands,
He who was conceived by the touching of two gloved hands.

Programme for an Emergency

The world's population, statistically,
Could stand together on the Isle of Wight
Shoulder to shoulder to shoulder.
There they could stand and watch the sea,
Sleeping in shifts by day and night,
Gracelessly growing older

But Holland's son would rape Ireland's daughter
Or China's grandfather fall in the water.
Ozone would mingle with the scent of slaughter.

Still, England seems the most suitable site,
For here we are proud not to laugh or weep
And one gulp of the air will freeze the strongest man in sleep.

So Don't Feed Your Dog Ordinary Meat, Feed Him Pal, Pal Meat for Dogs, P-A-L, Prolongs Active Life (Enriched with Nourishing Marrowbone Jelly)

My bird had a grin like a water-melon,
My bird was a hopeless case.
She wanted to look like Elvis Presley
So she paid a man to wipe the smile off her face,

He was
My friend the plastic surgeon
Your friend the plastic surgeon
Your friendly neighbourhood plastic surgeon
(Enriched with nourishing marrowbone jelly).

My mate was a dirty little Fascist,
They shouted him down when he cursed the Jews,
And nobody recognized his patriotic motives
Till he hired a man to explain his views,

39

He got
My friend the public relations man
Your friend the PRO
Your friendly neighbourhood public relations man
(Enriched with nourishing marrowbone jelly).

My dad was a nervy sort of navvy
He insured his job and his life and me,
Fire, floor, suicide and acts of God,
And then he insured his insurance policy,

He paid
My friend the man from the Prudential
Your friend the man from the Pru
Your friendly neighbourhood man from the Prudential
(Enriched with nourishing marrowbone jelly).

My mum spent her life watching telly
Till the Epilogue told her that her soul would burn.
Now she's got peace of mind and she still does nothing
For she pays one-tenth of all we earn

To
My friend the Anglican clergyman
Your friend the clergyman
Your friendly neighbourhood Anglican clergyman
(Enriched with nourishing marrowbone jelly).

The plastic surgeon and the public relations man,
The man from the Prudential and the man from God –
Pals, pals, every one a pal.
P-A-L,
Prolongs Active Life
(Enriched with nourishing marrowbone jelly).

Time and Motion Study

Slow down the film. You see that bit.
Seven days old and no work done.
Two hands clutching nothing but air,
Two legs kicking nothing but air.
That yell. There's wasted energy there.
No use to himself, no good for the firm.
Make a note of that.

New film. Now look, now he's fourteen.
Work out the energy required
To make him grow that tall.
It could have been used
It could have all been used
For the good of the firm and he could have stayed small.
Make a note of that.

Age thirty. And the waste continues.
Using his legs for walking. Tiring
His mouth with talking and eating. Twitching.
Slow it down. Reproducing? I see.
All, I suppose, for the good of the firm.
But he'd better change methods. Yes, he'd better.
Look at the waste of time and emotion,
Look at the waste. Look. Look.
And make a note of that.

Nostalgia – Now Threepence Off

Where are they now, the heroes of furry-paged books and comics brighter than life which packed my inklined desk in days when BOP meant Boys' Own Paper, where are they anyway?

Where is Percy F. Westerman? Where are H. L. Gee and Arthur Mee? Where is Edgar Rice (The Warlord of Mars), Burroughs, the Bumper Fun Book and the Wag's Handbook? Where is the Wonder Book of Reptiles? Where the hell is The Boy's Book of Bacteriological Warfare?

Where are the Beacon Readers? Did Ro-ver, that tireless hound, devour his mon-o-syll-ab-ic-all-y correct family? Did Little Black Sambo and Epaminondas shout for Black Power?

Did Peter Rabbit get his when myxomatosis came round the second time, did the Flopsy Bunnies stiffen to a standstill, grow bug-eyed, fly-covered and then disintegrate?

Where is G. A. Henty and his historical lads – Wolfgang the Hittite, Armpit the Young Viking, Cyril who lived in Sodom? Where are their uncorrupted bodies and Empire-building brains, England needs them, the *Sunday Times* says so.

There is news from Strewelpeter mob. Johnny-Head-In-Air spends his days reporting flying saucers, the telephone receiver never cools from the heat of his hand. Little Harriet, who played with matches, still burns, but not with fire. The Scissorman is everywhere.

Barbar the Elephant turned the jungle into a garden city. But things went wrong. John and Susan, Titty and Roger, became unaccountably afraid of water, sold their dinghies, all married each other, live in a bombed-out cinema on surgical spirits and weeds of all kinds.

Snow White was in the *News of the World* – Virgin Lived With Seven Midgets, Court Told. And in the psychiatric ward an old woman dribbles as she mumbles about a family of human bears, they ate porridge, yes Miss Goldilocks of course they did.

Hans Brinker vainly whirled his silver skates round his head as the jackboots of Emil and the Detectives invaded his Resistance Cellar.

Some failed. Desperate Dan and Meddlesome Matty and Strang the Terrible and Korky the Cat killed themselves with free gifts in a back room at the Peter Pan Club because they were impotent, like us. Their audience, the senile Chums of Red Circle School, still wearing for reasons of loyalty and lust the tatters of their uniforms, voted that exhibition a super wheeze.

Some succeeded. Tom Sawyer's heart has cooled, his ingenuity flowers at Cape Kennedy.

But they are all trodden on, the old familiar faces, so at the rising of the sun and the going down of the ditto I remember I remember the house where I was taught to play up play up and play the game though nobody told me what the game was, but we know now, don't we, we know what the game is, but lives of great men all remind us we can make our lives sublime and departing leave behind us arseprints on the sands of time, but the tide's come up, the castles are washed down, where are they now, where are they, where are the deep shelters? There are no deep shelters. Biggles may drop it, Worrals of the Wraf may press the button. So, Billy and Bessie Bunter, prepare for the last and cosmic Yarooh and throw away the Man-Tan. The sky will soon be full of suns.

Four for Children

Four for Children

The elephant knocked the ground with a stick,
He knocked it slow, he knocked it quick.
He knocked it till his trunk turned black—
Then the ground turned round and knocked him back.

If I had a rusty concrete mixer
I would fill it with Murcheson's Cough Elixir.
Doesn't the thought of it make you sick, sir?

Lovers lie around in it.
Broken glass is found in it
Grass
I like that stuff

Tuna fish get trapped in it
Legs come wrapped in it
Nylon
I like that stuff

Eskimos and tramps chew it
Madame Tussaud gave status to it
Wax
I like that stuff

Elephants get sprayed with it
Scotch is made with it
Water
I like that stuff

Clergy are dumbfounded by it
Bones are surrounded by it
Flesh
I like that stuff

Harps are strung with it
Mattresses are sprung with it
Wire
I like that stuff

Carpenters make cots of it
Undertakers use lots of it
Wood
I like that stuff

Cigarettes are lit by it
Pensioners get happy when they sit by it
Fire
I like that stuff

Dankworth's alto is made of it, most of it,
Scoobdedoo is composed of it
Plastic
I like that stuff

Man made fibres and raw materials
Old rolled gold and breakfast cereals
Platinum linoleum
I like that stuff

Skin on my hands
Hair on my head
Toenails on my feet
And linen on my bed

Well I like that stuff
Yes I like that stuff
The earth
Is made of earth
And I like that stuff

The runaway train knocked the buffers flat :
'Hey,' said the stationmaster, 'that's enough of that.
I've been forty-two years at this station
And I've never seen such bufferation.'

War

Fifteen Million Plastic Bags

I was walking in a government warehouse
Where the daylight never goes.
I saw fifteen million plastic bags
Hanging in a thousand rows.

Five million bags were six feet long
Five million bags were five foot five
Five million were stamped with Mickey Mouse
And they came in a smaller size.

Were they for guns or uniforms
Or a dirty kind of party game?
Then I saw each bag had a number
And every bag bore a name.

And five million bags were six feet long
Five million were five foot five
Five million were stamped with Mickey Mouse
And they came in a smaller size

So I've taken my bag from the hanger
And I've pulled it over my head
And I'll wait for the priest to zip it
So the radiation won't spread

Now five million bags are six feet long
Five million are five foot five
Five million are stamped with Mickey Mouse
And they come in a smaller size.

Lord Home Gets £5,000 a Year

Lord Home, Lord Home has an oblong face
Not beautifully designed and not plug-ugly
But bland, bland, a mirror of the times.
And Lord Home's bland and oblong face
Comes from a long line of bland and oblong faces.
Well-bred, says his tailor, wielding a cunning pair of scissors
Expensively for Lord Home, who was expensive to cultivate.
Now the money has been spent irretrievably,
Lord Home has been educated, brought forward, inspected,
    approved,
The worthy product of a long line
Of worthy products.

Lord Home, Lord Home, began to open
The mouth in his oblong face.
His mouth began to open and it continued opening until it was
    half-open, quite open, wide open –
A clean, chlorophylled cavern suitable for conversion into a
    shelter.
From the cavern crawled words in English which said the
    English love Berlin,
You remember that city when its forelock was black, a
    swastika at the centre of each eyeball, that city when each
    large eye wept rubble and the bodies of people Jewish and
    Gentile,
He said that for love of that city the British are prepared to be
    blown into atomic dust,
But, he said, remember he said but, he said but, but he said,
    but –
They would rather not.

Lord Home, Lord Home is a coward, a man without the guts
  of a chicken,
Unworthy of the line of oblong, dusty faces.
For I want to be dust, to be democracy-loving, free-enterprise
  dust.
Every damp atom in my body cries for dessication.
After the blast and the firestorm all my British atoms
Will patriotically assemble on the site where my heart once
  stood
To form a small, malicious cloud.
After the blast and after the firestorm
This army of atoms which once I used for living
Will wait in mindless patience for an easterly wind
To carry the cloud over the pelmets of the iron curtain
To rain steadily down on Moscow,
Maiming the bad men, the bad women and the bad children of
  Russia.

Order Me a Transparent Coffin
and Dig My Crazy Grave

After the next war ... and the sky
Heaves with contaminated rain.
End to end our bodies lie
Round the world and back again.

Now from their concrete suites below
Statesmen demurely emanate,
And down the line of millions go
To see the people lie in state.

Nikita Ikes, Franco de Gaulles,
Officiate and dig the holes.
Mao tse-Sheks, Macadenauers,
Toting artificial flowers.

As they pay tribute each one wishes
The rain was less like tears, less hot, less thick.
They mutter, wise as blind white fishes,
Occasionally they are sick.

But I drily grin from my perspex coffin
As they trudge till they melt into the wet,
And I say : 'Keep on walking, keep on walking,
You bastards, you've got a hell of a way to walk yet.'

A Child is Singing

A child is singing
And nobody listening
But the child who is singing :

Bulldozers grab the earth and shower it.
The house is on fire.
Gardeners wet the earth and flower it.
The house is on fire,
The houses are on fire.
Fetch the fire engine, the fire engine's on fire.
We will have to hide in a hole.
We will burn slow like coal.
All the people are on fire.

And a child is singing
And nobody listening
But the child who is singing.

The Dust

Singing, as she always must,
Like the kitten-drowner with a howling sack,
Open-eyed through the shallow dust
Goes the dust-coloured girl with a child on her back.

A schoolgirl in a flowered dress,
Swayed by the swaying of a tree
And the sun's grin, in front of her family
One day became a prophetess.

Like a singer who forgets her song
She awkwardly leant from the graceful chair,
Balanced her fists in the drawing-room air
And said that everyone was wrong, that she was wrong.

Shocked by this infantile mistake
Her uncles and aunts were sad to find
This ugly girl with an ugly mind
In a house as rich as birthday cake.

When the bombs fell, she was sitting with her man,
Straight and white in the family pew.
While in her the bud of a child grew
The city crumbled, the deaths began.

Now, singing as she always must,
A refugee from a love burned black,
Open-eyed through the rising dust
Goes the dust-coloured girl with a child on her back.

Veteran with a Head Wound

Nothing to show for it at first
But dreams and shivering, a few mistakes.
Shapes lounged around his mind chatting of murder,
Telling interminable jokes,
Watching like tourists for Vesuvius to burst.

He started listening. Too engrossed to think,
He let his body move in jerks,
Talked just to prove himself alive, grew thin,
Lost five jobs in eleven weeks,
Then started drinking, blamed it on the drink.

He'd seen a woman, belly tattered, run
Her last yards. He had seen a fat
Friend roll in flames, as if his blood were paraffin,
And herded enemies waiting to be shot
Stand looking straight into the sun.

They couldn't let him rot in the heat
In the corner of England like a garden chair.
A handy-man will take a weathered chair,
Smooth it, lay on a glowing layer
Of paint and tie a cushion to the seat.

They did all anyone could do—
Tried to grate off the colour of his trouble,
Brighten him up a bit. His rare
Visitors found him still uncomfortable.
The old crimson paint showed through.

Each night he heard from the back of his head,
As he was learning to sleep again,
Funny or terrible voices tell
Or ask him how their deaths began.
These are the broadcasts of the dead.

One voice became a plaintive bore.
It could only remember the grain and shine
Of a wooden floor, the forest smell
Of its fine surface. The voice rasped on
For hours about that pretty floor.

'If I could make that floor again,'
The voice insisted, over and over,
'The floor on which I died,' it said,
'Then I could stand on it for ever
Letting the scent of polish lap my brain.'

He became Boswell to the dead.
In cruel script their deaths are written.
Generously they are fed
In that compound for the forgotten,
His crowded, welcoming head.

The doctors had seen grimmer cases.
They found his eyes were one-way mirrors,
So they could easily look in
While he could only see his terrors,
Reflections of those shuttered faces.

Stepping as far back as I dare,
(For the man may stagger and be broken
Like a bombed factory or hospital),
I see his uniform is woven
Of blood, bone, flesh and hair.

Populated by the simple dead,
This soldier, in his happy dreams,
Is killed before he kills at all.
Bad tenant that he is, I give him room;
He is the weeper in my head.

Since London's next bomb will tear
Her body in its final rape,
New York and Moscow's ashes look the same
And Europe go down like a battleship,
Why should one soldier make me care?

Ignore him or grant him a moment's sadness.
He walks the burning tarmac road
To the asylum built with bricks of flame.
Abandon him and you must make your own
House of incinerating madness.

The horizon is only paces away.
We walk an alley through a dark,
Criminal city. None can pass.
We would have to make love, fight or speak
If we met someone travelling the other way.

A tree finds its proportions without aid.
Dogs are not tutored to be fond.
Penny-size frogs traverse the grass
To the civilization of a pond.
Grass withers yearly, is re-made.

Trees become crosses because man is born.
Dogs may be taught to shrink from any hand.
Dead frogs instruct the scientist;
Spread clouds of poison in the pond—
You kill their floating globes of spawn.

In London, where the trees are lean,
The banners of the grass are raised.
Grass feeds the butcher and the beast,
But we could conjure down a blaze
Would scour the world of the colour green.

For look, though the human soil is tough,
Our state scratches itself in bed
And a thousand are pierced by its fingernails.
It combs its hair, a thousand good and bad
Fall away like discs of dandruff.

For a moment it closes its careful fist
And, keening for the world of streets,
More sons of God whisper in jails
Where the unloved the unloved meet.
The days close round them like a dirty mist.

When death covers England with a sheet
Of red and silver fire, who'll mourn the state,
Though some will live and some bear children
And some of the children born in hate
May be both lovely and complete?

Try to distract this soldier's mind
From his distraction. Under the powdered buildings
He lies alive, still shouting,
With his brothers and sisters and perhaps his children,
While we bury all the dead people we can find.